THE BEST BOOK OF

Ancient Rome

Deborah Murrell

KINGFISHER

BOSTON

Contents

KINGFISHER

a Houghton Mifflin Company imprint
222 Berkeley Street
Boston, Massachusetts 02116
www.houghtonmifflinbooks.com

Created for Kingfisher Publications Plc
by Picthall & Gunzi Limited

Author and editor: Deborah Murrell
Designer: Dominic Zwemmer
Consultant: Richard Platt

Illustrators: Richard Hook, Adam Hook,
Angus McBride, Simoné Boni, Peter Dennis,
Les Edwards, Luigi Galante, David
Salariya, Ron Tiner, Thomas Trojer

First published in 2004

10 9 8 7 6 5 4 3 2 1

1TR/0304/WKT/MAR(MAR)/128KMA

Copyright © Kingfisher
Publications Plc 2004

LIBRARY OF CONGRESS CATALOGING-IN-PUBLICATION DATA
Murrell, Deborah Jane, 1963–
  The best book of ancient Rome/
  Deborah Jane Murrell.—1st ed.
  p. cm.
  Includes index.
  1. Rome—Social life and customs—Juvenile
literature. 2. Rome—History—Juvenile literature. [1.
Rome—History—Republic, 510-30 B.C.] I. Title.
  DG78.M87 2004
  937'.602—dc22
  2003027294

ISBN 0-7534-5756-3

Printed in China.

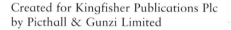

How Rome began

Around 3,000 years ago a tribe of people called the Latins settled on the hills where Rome, Italy, stands today. They had chosen a good place to live. From the top of the hills they could easily see any enemies approaching. The Tiber river below supplied fresh water, and they could reach the sea by boat. Soon more villages developed nearby, and eventually they all joined together to form the city of Rome.

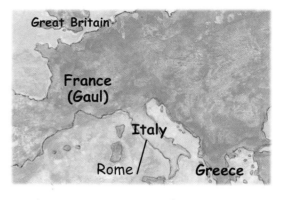

Where was early Rome?

Rome was on a fertile plain in Latium, a part of what is now Italy. To the north of Rome lived the Etruscans, and to the south lived a colony of Greek people. There were also smaller tribes of hill farmers, including the Sabines and the Samnites.

Tiber river

The hills of Rome

Rome is said to be built on seven hills. One of them, the Palatine hill, was probably the site of the first Latin villages. Later the emperors of Rome built their grand homes there. The word "palace" comes from the name of the Palatine hill.

The Etruscan enemy

The early Romans learned a lot from their powerful neighbors. The Greeks taught them science, architecture, and the arts. The Etruscans introduced them to gladiators, chariot races, and wearing a toga. The Etruscans often attacked Rome, and by around 600 B.C. the city was under Etruscan control. Historians believe that the last three kings of Rome were Etruscans.

Etruscan warriors attacked many Roman villages.

The Capitoline hill, below, is the center of government in modern Rome.

Early farmers grew grains, vegetables, and fruits.

Farmers used simple plows to prepare the land for planting.

Roman rulers

The first rulers of Rome were all kings. A group of men called senes, or senators, elected each king and advised him during his reign. According to some historians, there were seven Roman kings in total, and the last three were Etruscans, although nobody is certain. The last king, Tarquinius II, was overthrown in around 510 B.C., and Rome became a republic.

Tarquin the Proud

King Tarquinius II was also known as Tarquinius Superbus, which means "the proud." A Roman historian named Livy said that the king was very unpopular. Eventually the people of Rome drove the whole royal family out of the city.

Paying the price

There were 300 members of the Senate, all men from the richest families, who were known as patricians. Senators were expected to pay for things such as public buildings and entertaining people. Some of them spent so much money that they became bankrupt!

A tribune could stop any official act by saying "veto," meaning "I forbid."

People power

People who were not patricians were known as plebeians. Some plebeians felt it was unfair that only patricians could be senators. In 494 B.C. they threatened to leave Rome unless changes were made. So the Senate granted them their own council, with tribunes to speak for them. Later they gained the power of veto.

Hot topics

Some Romans, such as Cicero, were great orators, or public speakers. They could win support for their side of the argument by using their words alone. Debates in the Senate could become very heated!

The senators held debates in the Senate.

Senators usually wore togas for formal occasions.

The city of Rome

At the heart of the republic—and later the empire—was the city of Rome itself. Its public buildings were designed to be both practical and pleasing to look at. For example, the Forum Romanum was used as a market and as a meeting place. It also had a platform for people to make public speeches. Many of ancient Rome's buildings, such as the Colosseum and the Pantheon, are still standing today.

City in flames

Most city people lived in apartment buildings, with fires for heating, so there were often outbreaks of fires. Once people accused Emperor Nero of starting a fire just so that he could build a huge palace in the space left behind!

Trajan's Forum

Basilica Julia

Theater of Marcellus

Tiber river

Under the ground

Beneath the many temples of Rome
were large vaults, which some people
used to keep their money safe.
Burials were not allowed inside
the city, so the early Christians
dug catacombs under the ground
just outside the city limits so that
they could bury their dead.

Colosseum

Temple of Venus
and Rome

Aqua Claudia

Circus Maximus

Conquering new lands

The Roman republic had enemies on all sides. Some of the Latin cities formed a league to help each other fight the mountain tribes, and Rome joined it. By around 400 B.C. Rome had a great deal of land and was the strongest city in the league. Even though other tribes, such as the Gauls, regularly attacked Rome, the republic continued to expand. By 264 B.C. the Romans controlled all of Italy.

Auxiliary troops

The Roman army conquered many other lands and also recruited local soldiers from the armies that they had fought. These soldiers, called auxiliaries, were useful because they knew the area well. They defended Rome's new borders.

The Battle of Zama was fought in 202 B.C.

Carthaginian archers

Hannibal is humbled

From 264 B.C. the Roman army fought a series of wars with the Carthaginians from north Africa. In 218 B.C. the Carthaginian general Hannibal invaded Italy with 35,000 men and more than 30 elephants. He won battle after battle, but the Romans finally defeated him in Zama. In 146 B.C. Rome burned Carthage to the ground.

Roman legionaries

Building an empire

The Roman borders continued to expand. However, fights among Rome's leaders soon turned into civil war. In 49 B.C. Julius Caesar took control of Rome, and in 44 B.C. he became dictator for life. But soon he was murdered, and war broke out again. In 27 B.C. Caesar's adopted son, Octavian, became the first Roman emperor and was given the name Augustus.

Caesar on campaign

Julius Caesar was a brilliant politician and general. He fought many campaigns in Gaul and elsewhere from 58 B.C. to 49 B.C., and he extended Rome's borders as far as the English Channel.

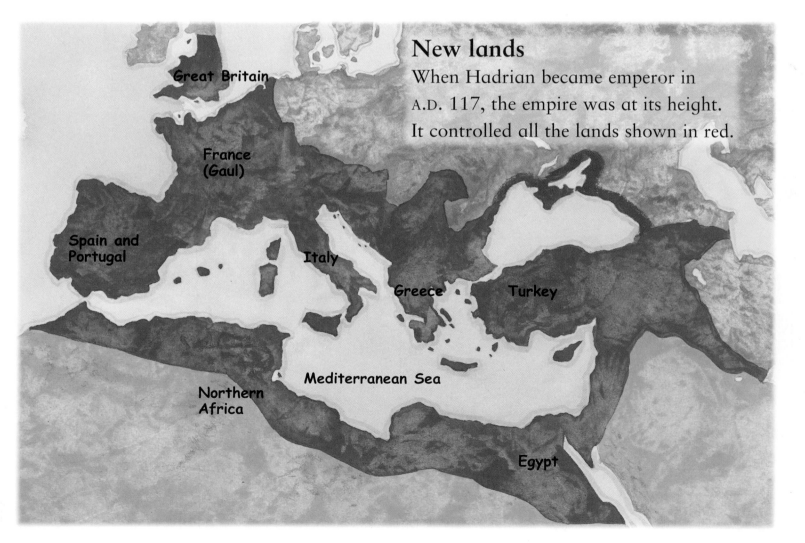

New lands

When Hadrian became emperor in A.D. 117, the empire was at its height. It controlled all the lands shown in red.

Great Britain

France (Gaul)

Spain and Portugal

Italy

Greece

Turkey

Mediterranean Sea

Northern Africa

Egypt

The Romans and
local tribes usually
fought on foot.

Hadrian's wall

The Romans conquered
Great Britain in A.D. 43.
Later Emperor Hadrian
built a huge wall to help the
army stop northern tribes
from invading Great Britain.
Some parts of the wall and its
towers are still standing today.

Hadrian's wall is 73 mi. long.

Controlling the tribes

The Roman borders were
constantly threatened by
local tribes. Many of the
tribes had so few weapons
that they were unlikely to
beat the mighty Roman
army. However, they fought
bravely and sometimes won
astonishing victories.

13

Army life

Rome's early army was made up of unpaid, untrained men. They were called to fight when they were needed, and most had to provide their own weapons. By the 2nd century B.C. the army had become a highly trained, professional force. Each man was paid and was given a set of weapons. When soldiers were not fighting, they spent most of their time training. Most were foot soldiers, but there were also soldiers on horseback—called the cavalry.

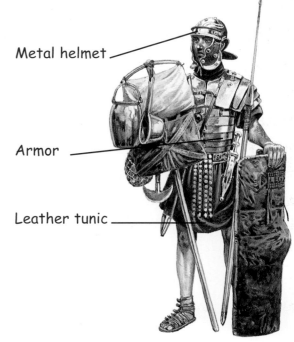

Metal helmet

Armor

Leather tunic

A legionary's weapons

Legionaries, or foot soldiers, used a short sword for stabbing and a javelin for throwing. Each soldier also carried a large shield and wore metal armor for protection.

The tortoise

When approaching an enemy, groups of Roman soldiers often formed a tortoise shape—called a testudo. They held their shields over their heads and around the sides of the group. This formation helped protect them from enemy missiles.

Military forts

In the early days of the empire the Romans began to build permanent forts to protect their empire's borders. All the forts had the same plan, so when soldiers had to move from one fort to another, it was very easy to find their way around the new one.

Cilurnum, a Roman military fort, was located in Chester, Great Britain.

Javelins made of iron and wood

Roman soldiers used shields made from wood and metal covered in leather.

15

Daily life in Rome

For the richest families life in ancient Rome was easy. They had large houses, good food, and slaves to do their work for them. But because slaves did most of the work, paid jobs were difficult to find. Many ordinary people had no way to earn a living. Some Romans were so poor that they could not survive without help. Toward the end of the republic the government regularly gave free corn to the poor people of the city of Rome.

Trade

Some people earned money by trading. Ships brought trade goods from the Mediterranean area and beyond. These included basic items, such as wool and corn, and luxuries such as amber.

A Roman merchant ship

Earning a living

Most people had to earn a living to feed themselves and their families. Some people made and sold food, clothes, or other goods. Others provided services such as secretarial work.

Roman shops sold all types of everyday items.

Big ships could not sail up the Tiber river to Rome but had to deliver their goods to Ostia, a large nearby seaport.

A slave auction

The rich Romans used slaves to farm their land and to clean their houses. They bought them at auctions, like the one shown here. Some Romans were kind to their slaves and sometimes even set the most loyal and faithful ones free. However, many treated their slaves very badly and beat them.

Slaves were sold at auctions.

17

In the home

Most Romans lived and worked in the country.

People in cities and towns usually lived in blocks of apartments, called insulae, with a few pieces of basic furniture. Rich families owned large homes and often had a town house as well as a country villa. Roman villas were usually set in large grounds, which the owners farmed. A grand home often had fine mosaics and other decorations on the floors and walls.

Rich people often owned a town house, like this one.

Hole in roof to let in light

Bedroom

Atrium

Many teachers were Greek slaves.

Shopkeepers often rented the rooms next to the street.

A little learning

Boys from wealthy families were well educated. They learned how to read, write, and count, either at home or in a school—called a ludus. Girls, however, usually only learned how to spin, weave, and sew.

Garden, or peristylium

Luxury living

The first room that guests entered when visiting a luxury town house was a large open space called an atrium. Most of the other rooms of the house were arranged around the atrium.

Dining room, or triclinium

Kitchen, or culina

Mosaic floor

Roman doctors

The ancient Romans did not really know why people became sick. Doctors tried their best to cure people using herbal medicines and sometimes gave them advice about the benefits of having a good diet and exercising.

Decorative pool, or impluvium

Doctors only made house calls to the rich.

Time to spare

The citizens of ancient Rome had a lot of spare time. The normal working day began in the early morning and ended at noon. There were around 100 days in the year when most people did not work at all. Rome's rulers provided many types of entertainment, and some of them were free so that even poor people could have a good time!

Public baths

Most Romans did not have a bathroom at home, so those who lived in a town or city used the public baths. In these baths they could get clean and exercise or relax with their friends.

At the theater

Roman people loved going to the theater. They laughed at comedies and cried at tragedies. The actors wore masks and colorful robes so that the audience could recognize the characters even from the back row.

Slaves brought food from the kitchen.

A feast fit for a king

Eating could be a big social event in Rome,
especially for the rich. Guests lay on couches
around low tables and ate right from the
serving dishes. Noble families tried to impress
each other by having the best dinner parties.

People usually ate
with their fingers.

21

Gladiators and wild beasts

At the arena there were wild animal fights in the morning and gladiator fights in the afternoon. The gladiators fought with various weapons, often to the death. However, a wounded gladiator could ask for mercy, and sometimes it was granted.

A myrmillon had a short sword and a rectangular shield.

A Thracian had a curved dagger and a small, square shield.

A retiarius had a trident and a net.

A Samnite had a short sword and a long, curved shield.

Sports and leisure

Sports in ancient Rome were different from those today. They were more dangerous, and many of the people who took part were forced to do so. Most of them were slaves, criminals, or enemy soldiers. To begin with, gladiator fights and chariot races were only held on special days. But they were so popular that Rome's rulers decided to have them more often!

A day at the races

At chariot races teams of drivers, chariots, and horses competed. They hurtled around the oval racetrack seven times, with chariots falling over and horses and people getting hurt or even killed. The fans sometimes became so excited that they began fighting each other!

Spartacus

In the 1st century B.C. a Thracian soldier named Spartacus was sold as a gladiator. He escaped and formed a large army of slaves. They resisted many attacks by Roman troops but were defeated when they invaded Rome.

The Circus Maximus was the biggest racetrack in the empire—and larger than any sports stadium built since then!

The fall of the empire

By the A.D. 300s the Roman Empire was in serious trouble. Disease, hunger, rising prices, civil unrest, and invasions all had a terrible effect. In A.D 395 the empire split permanently in half. The Western empire only lasted until A.D. 476, when it was conquered by Odoacer, a Germanic warrior. The Eastern empire, known as the Byzantine Empire, survived for almost another 1,000 years.

Emperor Constantine

By the time of Constantine in the A.D. 300s the empire had been split in half. Constantine reunited the two halves of the empire but moved its capital from Rome to Byzantium, which he renamed Constantinople.

Vandals overrun Rome

The city of Rome had its own special fighting force called the Praetorian Guard. But when the Vandals, from northern Europe, invaded in A.D. 455, the guardians were unable to stop them!

Constantinople topples

The Eastern empire survived until 1453, when Turkish Muslims attacked Constantinople. There were around ten times more attackers than defenders, and the city fell. The last part of the empire was then defeated.

The Vandals ransacked Rome for several days, taking valuable objects such as gold and bronze.

25

The legacy of Rome

Ancient Rome still affects our lives today.
The republican governments in the U.S. and France are based on the Roman republic, and the U.S. even has a Senate and senators. Many modern European languages, such as French and Spanish, are based on Latin, the language of the ancient Romans. Even the calendar that we use was invented during Julius Caesar's reign!

Roman aqueducts, which were built for carrying water, still stand all over Europe.

Romans building an aqueduct

Built to last

The Romans built things to last, and much of their work still survives. Other people have copied the Roman style, and towns and cities all over the world have buildings like those of ancient Rome.

Building a Roman road

1 First the road builders dug a trench and removed all the loose soil and rocks. This gave them a solid surface to work on.

2 Then the builders poured in layers of fine, dry soil and small stones. The road was highest in the middle to help drain water.

3 The next layer contained a type of concrete made of broken stones and lime. This was followed by a layer of gravel or sand.

4 Finally smooth, flat stone slabs were laid on top. The hard-wearing surface that they formed often lasted for many centuries.

Famous Romans

Many Romans were famous for being great soldiers or emperors, like these men on the right. But there were also Romans who became famous for other talents—such as acting, singing, writing, or great sportsmanship!

Julius Caesar c. 100-44 B.C. A dictator for life from 45 B.C. and murdered in 44 B.C.

Augustus 63 B.C.–A.D. 14 The first emperor, who ruled wisely and improved the capital.

Hadrian A.D. 76-138 An emperor who built huge forts and walls to protect the empire.

Constantine the Great c. A.D. 274-337 A Christian emperor who reunited the two halves of the empire.

27

Mount Vesuvius

The destruction of Pompeii

In A.D. 79 a volcano called Mount Vesuvius erupted in a huge explosion. Buildings in the nearby city of Pompeii were destroyed, and many people and animals died. In the 1700s archaeologists uncovering the city found that the ash had preserved many items perfectly.

Many objects, such as money, jewelry, and food, were found in Pompeii.

Some of the uncovered buildings still had brightly colored walls.

Objects found in Pompeii

A Roman gladiator's helmet

A preserved loaf of bread

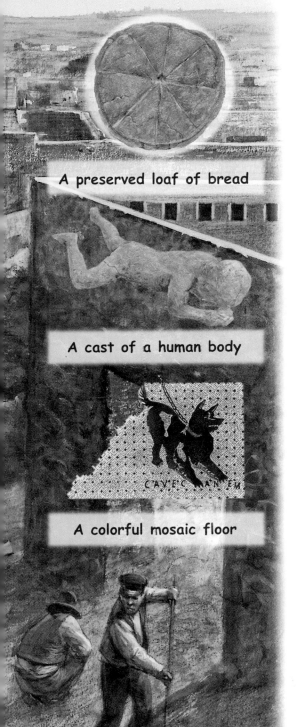

A cast of a human body

A colorful mosaic floor

How do we know?

We know a great deal about ancient Rome from the writers of the time. Most of the original writing is lost, but in the late empire people began to make copies of the works of ancient Roman historians, poets, and other writers. We can also learn from the work of archaeologists, who look at the remains of settlements and the items found there and figure out how people lived at the time.

Shipwrecks

On the ocean floor marine archaeologists have discovered the remains of Roman ships. These can tell us what types of goods they were carrying such as the amphora, or container, above. We can also learn about how the ships were made and how sailors lived.

Rome today

The city of Rome is the capital of modern-day Italy. It is the political and business center of the nation and is at the heart of tourism and culture. But in between the stores and modern offices there are still many ancient buildings. Children play among the columns of the Pantheon, and cars drive around Rome's most famous arena—the Colosseum.

Ancient and modern

This picture shows part of Rome today. Over time people have stripped the valuable outer layers off some of the oldest buildings to build new structures. Pollution and traffic vibrations have also badly damaged the old buildings.

The Colosseum

Glossary

amber Fossilised tree resin (sap), often used in jewelry.

amphora A container used for food, oil, and other items.

archaeologist A person who studies ancient objects and the remains of ancient sites to find out how people lived.

archer A soldier who fights using a bow and arrow.

arena The space where gladiators and other entertainers performed for an audience.

auction A sale where goods are sold to the person who is willing to pay the highest price.

cast Something that forms in the space that is left behind by another object.

catacomb An underground place with many tunnels where the early Christians who lived in ancient Rome buried their dead.

civil war A war fought between people of the same nation.

comedy A play that has a comic, or happy, ending.

dictator A ruler who has total control over his people.

empire A group of nations, usually ruled by the leader of the strongest nation.

general An army officer who is in command of many soldiers.

gladiator A person, usually male, trained to fight in an arena to entertain an audience.

league A group of people who all work for the same purpose.

patrician The head of one of the richest families in ancient Rome.

plebeian Any free person in Rome who was not a patrician.

politician A person who works as part of the government of a country or nation.

pollution Car fumes and other toxic substances that can harm people, animals, and buildings.

republic A nation whose rulers are elected by its people.

Senate A council of senators.

temple A building where people go to worship their god or gods.

toga A type of robe, worn draped around the body.

tragedy A play that has a tragic, or sad, ending.

tribune A person elected by the plebeians to speak in a council.

vault An underground room, often in a temple or a bank, where people store important items.

veto The power to prevent others from introducing a law or other rule.

Index